GUNPOWDER

GUNPOWDER

Bernard O'Donoghue

Chatto & Windus
LONDON

First published in 1995

1 3 5 7 9 10 8 6 4 2

Copyright © Bernard O'Donoghue 1995

Bernard O'Donoghue has asserted his right under the
Copyright, Designs and Patents Act, 1988 to be
identified as the author of this work

First published in Great Britain in 1995 by
Chatto & Windus Limited
Random House, 20 Vauxhall Bridge Road
London SW1V 2SA

Random House Australia (Pty) Limited
20 Alfred Street, Milsons Point, Sydney,
New South Wales 2061, Australia

Random House New Zealand Limited
18 Poland Road, Glenfield
Auckland 10, New Zealand

Random House South Africa (Pty) Limited
PO Box 337, Bergvlei, South Africa

Random House UK Limited Reg. No. 954009

A CIP catalogue record for this book is available from
the British Library

ISBN 0 7011 6331 3

Typeset by SX Composing Ltd, Rayleigh, Essex
Printed in Great Britain by
Mackays of Chatham PLC, Chatham, Kent

For Heather

"We owe to the Middle Ages the two worst inventions
of humanity – gunpowder and romantic love."
                                        André Maurois

Acknowledgments

Some of the Poems in this volume appeared in the earlier collections *Razorblades and Pencils* (Sycamore Press, 1984) and *The Absent Signifier* (Mandeville Press, 1990). Acknowledgments are also due to the editors of the following journals and magazines where other poems appeared for the first time: *Bosphorus, Illuminations, The Independent, The Irish Reporter, London Review of Books, New Statesman, The Observer, Oxford English, The Oxford Magazine, Oxford Poetry, New Poetry Quarterly, Poetry Review, Seanchas Dúthalla, The Southern Review, Tandem, Thumbscrew* and *The Times Literary Supplement*. I am very grateful to Alice Kettle for permission to use her textile for the cover.

Contents

THE RAINMAKER

In the café at Crewe, you can still feel
The old excitement of trains: a stranger's
Eye-contact, held guiltily too long.
But as the Bangor train-time approaches,
Gradually the glamorous melt away
For Lime Street, Euston or Piccadilly.
You take your seat alone, half-reading the paper.

At the second stop a man – knocking on:
Seventy if he's a day – steps carefully
Into the seat across from you,
With neat cap and blue Everton scarf.
He reaches inside his gaberdine mac
And pulls out a small book. I can see,
Without peering too obviously,
That it is the poems of Dafydd ap Gwilym
In Welsh. His lips begin to move;
His eyes never lift again. He must be
Going to Bangor too. Celtic Studies Dept.?
But no: at Colwyn Bay, above the caravans
And idle fairground stuff, he folds the book
Back inside his scarf and off he goes.

And at that moment – 4.30 p.m.,
On Friday January the thirteenth –
The bleared weather that had effaced
The long and horizontal English midlands
Gives way to reaching bird-filled shores
Where ringed plover vies with lapwing
To catch your eye against the latening sun.

THE IRON AGE BOAT AT CAUMATRUISH

If you doubt, you can put your fingers
In the holes where the oar-pegs went.
If you doubt still, look past its deep mooring
To the mountains that enfold the corrie's
Waterfall of lace through which, they say,
You can see out but not in.
If you doubt that, hear the falcon
Crying down from Gneeves Bog
Cut from the mountain-top. And if you doubt
After all these witnesses, no boat
Dredged back from the dead
Could make you believe.

LOUISBURGH

"Interest in the weather is only forgivable in
those who have to make a journey by sea"
                                    Gerald of Wales

Only one photograph caught the spring
Of moment when the wave splash-broke,
Throwing an iridescent screen
Of lace that the world was green behind
In west Mayo. Around the corner
Lobster-pots stood cold and empty
On the pier, up for cruelty,
Exercising their right of silence.
Below them in the stiller water
Gross orange jellyfish closed and opened,
Engine-valves slowed nearly to stopping.

Hold them. Freeze as well the picture
Of the curlew's call above the grotto-rocks
Of sugar-bag blue-grey, and we could spend
For ever here. But already, now,
In Ireland, the rain's eavesdropping
On the silence. Guilt is sitting on
The cracked guttering, as if he owned
The place, smirking, watching the drip.
Before we're round the fjord in Killary Harbour,
He'll have tightened his hold, our only thought
Of slipping slates and mortar's deliquescence.

THE FLOAT

Who would put iron wheels under
A hay-car? On the outward trip
Seed-motes, steel rope-hooks, children
Teeth-jagged, unbalanced
Trampolinists in a vacuum-chamber,
Two inches off the boards.

On the way back
A cream yeast-loaf, risen over
The sides, sliding backstage
Through fern-and-briar curtains
Into the past, as now in the mirror
The car seems to disappear
Through its own rear-window
Into the car-wash tresses.

HAVE THE GOOD WORD

Those modern gods, the concentration
Camp authorities, when they had stripped
You of your clothes, would ask if you
Had some saving skill which might outweigh
In value the lead fillings in your teeth:
If you could sew, or type, or translate
From one useful language to another.

What I could offer them is the ability
To tell people what they want to hear:
That they will win the war, or that
Their names will go down in history
With honour; or that, after their deaths,
Mourners will kneel at their neat suburban graves,
Leaving bouquets and plastic immortelles.

PASSIVE SMOKING

The cows' repulsive body-heat
Kept the car warm through frosty nights,
Making it easier to start
For its spattering push up the passage.
Even so, my father sat for minutes
Every morning and stared out
With the engine running
And the carbon monoxide folding
Into the blackthorn mist.

I loved it. I stood at the back,
Breathing deep the scented poison
While his gaze travelled up Murt's field
To the mountains beyond.
What he saw nearer I don't know:
A pheasant sometimes in November;
Occasionally a cold fox; a neighbour
Spraying a grey liquid across the hedge?
But always the inexorable
Brown-green, rain-infected mound.

CORONACH

No two told the story the same way,
Even afterwards. The Caseys, driving back
From a job above Rockchapel, as they did
Every day at that time, saw nothing
Unusual as they passed the house.
They said the light was on, the gate closed
Just like it always was. Whether there was
Smoke from the chimney, they couldn't say.

Leary's niece swears that she saw him lying
On his bike against a ditch, with one hand
Over his chest. She said nothing to him,
Thinking he was only out of breath, or drunk.
But as she hurried on, she thought she heard
Him saying, 'I'm fin.' She took one look back,
But he was still propping himself on the bike,
Against the ditch. Earlier in the day

He'd certainly been to the butcher and had bought
Two chops and half a pound of sausages,
As he often did. The butcher half-remembered
That he'd said something about the horse-fair
(Or maybe the pony-show was what he meant)
And talked about football. But the strange thing
Is the butcher said he'd certainly walked *down*
The street after leaving the shop. The woman said,

With equal certainty, that he'd walked up.
She remembered because he'd broken into a trot,
Something he never did. Two people independently
Confirmed his bike had been parked outside
The church. They couldn't have been wrong because
One mudguard was black and one was green. He
Was found with a prescription in his pocket,
But no-one saw him at the doctor's.

The blackbird sang at 4 a.m.;
The cattle shifted in the field.
An almost silent tapping sound
Could be heard from the gully
Under Lisrobin bridge.
Did he hear them, any of them,
As his blood cooled and his
Muscles set, fixing in his ears
And retina the sound
And scenery of his death?

PERSEIDS

The darkening shoreline cleared
As the first stars formed, so
Everyone went to the pub
To give the night a chance
To prepare its sky in peace
For these momentous guests.
Just after midnight, when
The meteor shower was forecast,
We came back out and waited
For our eyes to grow accustomed
To the dark, with our backs
To the smoked orange light
Indoors. But they never
Readjusted, however much
We strained and peered against
The cloudcover. And then
Large drops began to fall,
The first thunder to roll
In the distance. One by one
They jumped across us, breaking
Against the ground, to denote
The passing or coming
Of what wet soul who could say.

KILLING THE PIG

The hackneyed subject of this witch's pastime,
At least, should be uncontroversial:
No love lost for the grim man in the cap
Who supervised the degrading, upside-down
Pulleying upwards of the condemned beast –
Aghast, screaming, foaming with fear.
Unflinching, with his knife he seamed from nave
To chaps, choking with a skilled draw across
The throat the last cry that penetrated
The pillows over the ears of shattered children.

He drank his tea and took the time to blow up
The bladder into a light, ludicrous football;
Tut-tutted that his payment was too much
Before slipping you a coin with a hushing wink.

One memorable winter night he shot a stray
That had broken into the henhouse, causing panic.
He reported afterwards it wagged its tail
As he took aim. His other specialism
Was dishorning calves. Whatever *poison-twigs*
Means amid the heroics of *Beowulf*
(Damascened patterns, arsenic on sword-tip,
Or snake etchings), there was no mistaking
The wince in the calf's eye as the weeping stick
Of acid rolled gingerly into her skull.

He was only banished when he took the law
Into his own hands and hanged the dog
That ate the household's eggs. Not knowing what
To think, I watched him wrap his Sunday suit
With binder-twine and heard him muttering
"Do they want the place to go to rack and ruin?"

THE COURTESY STONE

Whether or not the stone
Was designed for delegated prayer,
That it is heartshaped now,
No-one can doubt (and yet
It *is* very like a camel).
As for praying, like living,
Our servants could do that for us;
Big farmers had no time for it,
Spring or harvest.

Go there and pray, then,
All you incurables: jobless,
Old, poor or sick. Kneel down
By the boulder: if there are
Rags enough, you must surely
Have trust in God.

I'd like to pray with you
Myself, but, not believing, can't.
So I depute those whose steady eyes
Never saw a stir from the virgin
At Ballinspittle, while she dipped
And bent, with the desperate appeal
Of an auditioning cabaret dancer,
For the quizzical appraisal
Of us, cafflers by the narrow gate.

THE SUGAWN ROAD

You're driving down the sugawn road,
Just before midnight, late July.
The mist from the Araglen below
Ribbons in white patches by.
Ahead you know, less than a mile,
Is the cross by Glash school, where
You have to turn left for home.
But, as the car hums through that air,
Suspended in the radio's music,
You might by fortune never reach it.

CEO DRAIOCHTA (MAGIC MIST)

Leary sniffed the sweating wheat
Which had heated in the rick
That heavy autumn, reluctant
To dirty the machine with it.
But thirty men were gathered in the yard
And two fences had been levelled
For the thresher's awkward entry,
So finally he shrugged
And withdrew to the kitchen.

Nothing went right all day. Twice
The zipping drum was choked by sheaves
That skidded from their tyings
So the engine growled to a halt.
The home farmer, hurrying,
Shouldered the drivebelt off
With his sack. And all through the day
The strange bright mist that the sun
Could not break through got heavier

And the gloss-painted orange boards
Got slippier. They were nearly finished,
The best made of a bad job, when Leary
Who'd been dozing by the fire until
He'd be called to end the operation,
Leapt to his feet, hearing two things:
The machine's bellow rapidly sinking
And a scream that those of us in school
That famous day heard from two miles away.

They ran in all directions.
John Tim Jack, seventeen stone,
Cleared two walls on his way home.
Our Tim crashed through the front door
And hid his face in his chaff-pierced sleeve
Crying. "Matt Bridgie slipped into the drum.
His leg was taken off from the knee down."

That was it really. A man passing
From town tied a belt around the leg
And administered a cigarette.
Pieces of rubber from the wellington
And clots of sock were scraped
From the hopper. Ultimately
Some compensation was paid, enough
For a rudimentary false leg
And a few rounds of drinks.
Matt showed signs of a latent
Family talent for composing verse,
And often sang well past closing-time.

NEL MEZZO DEL CAMMIN

No more overcoats; maybe another suit,
A comb or two, and that's my lot.
So the odd poem (two in a good year)
Won't do to make the kind of edifice
I'd hoped to leave. Flush out the fantasy:
The mid-point being passed, the pattern's clear.
This road I had taken for a good byway
Is the main thoroughfare; and even that
Now seems too costly to maintain.
Too many holes to fill; not enough time
To start again. "I wasn't ready. The sun
Was in my eyes. I thought we weren't counting."

Soon we'll be counting razorblades and pencils.

AMATEURS

After the Caseys drove their big V8
Into the station-gates and had to flee
The district, the best local mechanic
Was the tailor. He'd thrust his beret back,
Wind up his dim flashlamp and peer in hope
Under the bonnet. When mothers fretted
At school-hours lost for the want of a car,
He offered comfort: "what does it matter?
You're decent people; everyone respects you."

Why was it the pipers' band who ran
The carnival? In full uniform –
Kilt, sporran, cap and bulging yellow socks –
They manned bingo tables, rifle-ranges
And hoop-las. Their power was absolute:
If they wanted, they could give a prize
Even when your bamboo ring sat lurched
Across the base. The man who judged
The dancing had two national medals

For ploughing. The doctor had been trained
As a priest and then got doubts; the priest,
As it happened, was a doctor.
The woman who specialized in cutting
Seed-potatoes, one eye per plant,
Had a History degree. It all remains
A mystery, even today; the only
Explanation I can think of is
People must like doing something for a change.

WINTER

The season when, the cows being dry
And fields fallow, you use the time
To take stock of the tools: replace
The odd handle, sharpen a blade, or oil
An axle. Then wrap steel again
In a half-damp cloth, ready for action;
Like a thought, seeded down until
It can answer to the event
That has lain in waiting for it:
The hedge that needed trimming, or the gully
By the wayside that was choking
With the careless surplus of the previous summer.

IN VINO VERITAS

1

The Blythburgh misericord
Depicting drunkenness is
Featureless. A smooth plane
Fronts its cowl, honester
By two clear faces than 'Fair-Seeming';
Yet no art can read the mind's
Construction in this polished
Oaken medieval oval.

The Egyptians, according
To Herodotus, passed laws
When drunk at night, then
Reconsidered them sober
In the morning. But if they
Passed them sober, they met
To reconsider them in drink.
Herodotus adds "personally,
I don't believe this myself."

2

In wartime the gates of Janus,
Back and front, stand open
To the public: no dissembling
Then. But in our days of peace,
They're shut tight and guarded
By sober vigilantes.

Listen to the sad carousal
Of closing-time, each voice slurred
Suspiciously into every other.
Log them; expose such honest plans
As hatch behind those pickled knots
Where eyes should be. Then lower
The discreet seat and sit on it.
Bow your head in prayer, keeping
The soothsayer staring at the floor.

STEALING UP

I've always hated gardening: the way
The earth gets under your nails
And in the chevrons of your shoes.
So I don't plan it; I steal up on it,
Casually, until I find –
Hey presto! – the whole lawn's cut
Or the sycamore's wand suddenly
Sports an ungainly, foal-like leaf.

Similarly, I'd have written to you
Sooner, if I'd had the choice.
But morning after morning I woke up
To find the same clouds in the sky,
Disabling the heart. But tomorrow
Maybe I'll get up to find an envelope,
Sealed, addressed to you, propped against
My cup, lit by a slanting sun.

AUROFAC 20

The chemist's perfect hair and her scent of roses
As we drudged in on our farmer's errand,
Coughing inferiority. Pink lipsticks,
Sunglasses, kiss-curls on cards of hairgrips:
Exoticism, sweetening the imagination
In a wet March when stogged wellingtons
Were welded to mud. "The calves have scour, ma'am."

The smell of hayseed; thinking the echo
Of the hayfloat's stammering ratchet
Tuning in, then fading over the air.
That station, quick, again; lavender, pine
And blue-flush our stale reflections in the days
Of sprays of the scent of roses.

STAPLES

When first appointed, along with other
Lesser office necessaries, I bought
A strong stapler and an economy pack
Of five thousand staples. I felt sure
They'd see me out, and for years that seemed
A sound calculation; the red box
Stayed full or nearly full: so packed that,
If one block fell out, it took some skill
To slide it back again. But it's now
A few years since I first noticed them
Loosening and the box rattling
When I held it. I started on the quiet
To use the company's stapler
Whenever possible, to eke them out.
And then last week, with the few mini-blocks
Fast approaching countability,
With no warning, the stapler's hinge snapped.
Who would have thought, however numerous
Those spindly sigla were, they would outlast
The metal arm that banged them into place?

CAROLLING

We were terrible lucky to catch
The Ceaucescus' execution, being
By sheer chance that Christmas Day
In the only house for twenty miles
With satellite TV. We sat,
Cradling brandies, by the fire,
Watching those two small, cranky autocrats
Lying in snow against a blood-spattered wall,
Hardly able to believe our good fortune.
The picture wasn't all that clear,
But the reporter told us how
The cross woman's peasant origins
Came out at the last, shouting
At her executioners "I have been
A mother to you and this is how
You thank me for it". We switched over
To join in with the carols
On the blockbuster Christmas special
On the other side, thanking
The stars that had saved us, with no
Effort on our part, from such tyranny.

ORPHIC

Next time through, I'll have a better grasp
Of constellations and the names of birds.
When I come up from the underground
Into the light, I'll know exactly
What station I'm at and which way
I'm facing. On this present trip
There's been too much to learn; the pause
For thought has always caught me
Napping. I'll give you an example:

One spring morning on the way to work
I came upon this man with a white beard,
Waving a bottle at me, bawling out
"How many All Ireland medals has Jack Lynch?
More or less than Ring? If you make out
You're Irish, you'll know that." I did know
And I stopped to tell him, despite my fear
He was only after money. But I'd have been
(This is the real point) better employed

Boning up on economics, say, since
The next winter was a hard one
And it got him. Or not economics
Necessarily: any field of knowledge.
I could have made an impact, pointing through
The city light at Betelgeuse (alpha
In Orion), or at the tree where the thrush
Nested. But something always came
To distract me and make me turn aside.

STELLATA

Patient through the months of winter
The down on the magnolia bud
Toughs out its ugliness, sustained
By the hope that for one week
Of April stardom it will unfold
Its flimsy, useless flower,
By which time the pear-blossom
Will have already fallen,
Leaving only whiskered clusters
Of miniature pear-grotesques.

THE WISDOM OF SAVING

1

Coláiste Pádraig, Millstreet, Co.Cork,
Not being a public school, didn't go in
For prizes; the only thing I won
Was a pound token for an essay on
'The Wisdom of Saving'. To keep this pound
My sister gave me a pale blue box
With the Queen and Horse Guards on the cover,
Which in turn had been given to her
In remarkable circumstances:
A shopkeeper, Lily Justice, emptied it
Of biscuits because it could be locked
With a small silver key to keep its contents safe.

2

Stephen Sullivan gave me half-a-crown
The day he was laid off by his employer
Who sold the cows. I cried all day, biting
The sliotar he had left behind for me:
And yet it was my sister that he loved.
I later learned that his letters from East London
About West Ham and the Irish rugby team –
And the Welshman is no slouch – were covers
For his love-letters to her. I stored
The half-crown in the locked box for years
Until in an emergency I used it
To buy a first day cover stamp of Arthur Guinness.

3

Nature wastes nothing: a point that Enid Blyton
Makes by comparing the purple flower
Of the thistle to little shaving-brushes
Which an elf could use in an emergency.
The latest contents of the Horse Guards box
Are items salvaged from my father's pocket
When he died, suddenly, away from home:
A box of matches (Maguire and Patterson),
A handkerchief, and, for some odd reason,
A worn down shaving brush. I don't think now
That any new obsession will displace
Those. And they'll themselves be looked at less and less.

HEATHER

How noticeably she broke in
Upon my life, displacing
Its age-old denizens,
Family and fantasy.
Her hair no brushed sheen
But knuckled nuggets
Of twisted gules,
Sprung vibrant as her name-flower.

Not unaccompanied, but with a guest
Whose acquaintance is more often
Claimed than proved: a name
Much taken in vain.
Close the curtains, lest
The lamp she lit might pull
In from the summer night
Mysterious moths to make cotters in her hair.

CAEDMON

Far be it from me to start telling
The truth at this stage of my life;
But this, anyway, is how it happened.

Everyone but me had a partypiece
That they were known for: Denis's was
'The Working Man'; Katty in her eighties
Sang 'Bury me beneath the apple tree',
Protesting more with every year that passed.
Padraig Lynch looked down steadily
At sad visions in the far corner
Of the room and shook them from his pipes.

So every festive night – Christmas, Stations,
American Wake or threshing – I'd slip out
When the music started, and find something
To do around the yard: tighten a rope,
Check that the henhouse door was shut
Against the fox, or look over the gate
To see if the cattle had strayed
Out of their field: anything.

One cold March (I couldn't name the year)
I was out on an errand of the kind,
Hearing the thinned music smoking out
Through the lighted door. I was nudging,
For the want of something better, at the ribs
Of straw welded to the ground by frost,
When I saw that there was someone else
In the stall: a girl dressed in red
And green, with – maybe a trick of sight
Thrown by the cows' breath on the dark –
A nimbus enveloping her hair.

She reached (like this) her hand out, asking me:
"Come on, you sing something". "I can't", I said;
"That's why I came out here". "But wouldn't you
Sing one song for me before I go?"
"But what about?" "Take your note from me.
Sing about the locals here and how
The whole thing started: what put them
At the music." I closed my eyes and tried,
Seeing her through the lids nodding approval,
Her colour lilting slowly in the light.

Now I'm in demand at all the sessions:
Dan Connell's Fridays/Sundays; Scully's
Mondays; even Jury's sometimes.
And if I'm ever tempted in the least
To call it a day, I only have
To close my eyes and think back to her mission.

GOING UP ON DECK
for Steven Rose

Either because there's a finite number
Of viruses, most of which you've had
Already, or because your immune
System loses the stomach for the fight,
As you get older, you don't catch colds so much.

Nor do I any longer care about
That corner of the road, avoided
For twenty years because of the back
Of a navy coat. *We* could have foretold
That the heart grows old: we sped it on its way.

But isn't every kiss a Judas kiss,
Pointing the way ahead? You can't survive
For ever on the life-enhancing pain
Of the happy time recalled in misery;
Fireside warmth becomes as tantalizing

To the speckled shin. Twenty years
Is a good innings for nostalgia,
Before dedication wilts. Nowadays
I find myself inclined to linger
In the cabin's mild protection,

While affection cools for that fool
Who stood by the rail, inventing
A waving, waiting girl in a long scarf,
And seeking inspiration in the slung
Sack's smack against the solid sea,

Or verbalizing the waves' sweep by the side,
Imperious as the driving gannet. He's
There still, I'm sure, held in place by the dark
And the sudden wind at the corners,
And the chain's rattle in the lifeboat's throat.

ELIJAH ON HOREB

The dog stood in the middle of the kitchen,
Eyes shut, thin tongue panting, slaver falling
Copiously, as the thunder reloaded to blast
The window-frames again. She must have seen
The stray that worried sheep tied up and shot.
And the lord was not in that.

Danny Regan took to going to Mass
In his old age after a scrawny tree fell
In a November storm, crushing the car-bonnet
In front of him. For a week we lifted branches,
Reopening roads, still smelling the pine.
And the lord was not in that.

The day we climbed The Paps, we had been warned
Of rain moving in off the Atlantic.
Without explanation, it never came. We sat,
Sheltered by the summit-marking dug of stones,
Looking south-west to the inlet at Kenmare.
Then we moved out to feel the breeze's blessing.

WORK

When driving a cow, you must take care
To herd her through the right gap,
Or else she will dodge past
And before you know where you are,
She'll be back in the farmyard, chewing
And gazing contentedly at nothing.

COTTON-REEL TRACTORS

You started with an empty cotton-reel,
And then the melted butt-end of a candle
In which was wedged a long sherbet-stick,
Axled through the centre by a rubber band
To a tack hammered in the other side.
To stop it sliding on the varnished desk-wood,

You hacked out serrations in the rim – wooden,
Round, commercial – of the cotton-reel
So the machine lurched along the splintered side
Of an upturned butter box. The candles
Were lit one winter evening: a band
Of snow was spreading southwards and might stick,

According to the forecast. You'd gone for sticks
To the cypress-screen (our name for a wood)
Where, year in, year out, at Christmas the same band
Of tinkers camped. You'd seen them reeling
Late back from the pub, terrified that the candle
In your bedroom-window would show which side

Of the house you slept in: they slept outside
And scorned those children that would stick
With beds. But now a girl sat dicing a candle,
Placing each thin red ring on a wooden
Tray, like draughts, amid rows of cotton-reels
Of every girth and height, and rubber bands,

A deep web of them. One thin yellow band
Gripped her hair back, holding on one side
A gorsebush-like swatch. She'd just taken one reel
In her left hand when you dropped your sticks
And ran. She ran too, after you through the wood
Calling "Can you give us a Christmas candle

To light the cradle?" I could see the candle
Burning in our own indoors, and the warm band
Of heat under the door where the wood
Had warped on the colder eastern side.
She was crying now and calling "This stick's
For you, to make the best ever tractor-reel."

But you escaped, your head reeling. By the side
Of the wood-road next morning, just some sticks
In the swaddling-band of snow, and one perfect candle.

GUNPOWDER

In the weeks afterwards, his jacket hung
Behind the door in the room we called
His study, where the bikes and wellingtons
Were kept. No-one went near it, until
Late one evening I thought I'd throw it out.
The sleeves smelt of gunpowder, evoking . . .
Celebration – excitement – things like that,
Not destruction. What was it he shot at
And missed that time? A cock pheasant
That he hesitated too long over
In case it was a hen? The rat behind
The piggery that, startled by the bang,
Turned round to look before going home to its hole?

Once a neighbour who had winged a crow
Tied it to a pike thrust in the ground
To keep the others off the corn. It worked well,
Flapping and cawing, till my father
Cut it loose. Even more puzzlingly,
He once took a wounded rabbit off the dog
And pushed it back into the warren
Which undermined the wall. As for
Used cartridges, they stood well on desks,
Upright on their graven golden ends,
Supporting his fountain-pen so that
The ink wouldn't seep into his pocket.

PILGRIMS

We're never only driving to the sea,
But also on the watch for dippers,
Red-berried holly, bagged turf
Or logs to burn, though we rarely
Find what we are looking for.
The most familiar roadsigns are to places
We've never been: 'O'Grady's Hold';
'The Earl of Desmond's Monument';
'The Boathouse at Laugharne'.

On childhood trips to Ballybunion
We always bypassed 'Mountcollins a quarter'.
But recently, thinking I'd time to spare,
I did turn for Mountcollins, finding it
A hilly village of narrow bridges
Over a stony river where you might well
See dippers: a place that in Italy
Would have been made picturesque
With hanging baskets and umber rooftiles.

I noted trailers there with outsize,
Mud-caked tyres: also powerlines sagging
Over the road. And then I drove on,
As though pursuing love and knowledge like
Some medieval pilgrim who, not resting
At the long-imagined shrine, obdures
In curiosity, wanting wonders:
The Great Khan or Prester John or Juggernaut.
But what I found when I left Mountcollins was

That the sick friend I should have been hurrying
To visit, had left already
To winter on the coastline further north.

THE YOUNGEST IN THE CLASS

Heroes were rarely young in modern Ireland.
The nearest some of us got to glory
Was to be the youngest in the class,
Complacently overhearing praise:
"They all had great brains, the Donoghues.
His Auntie Ellie the teacher
Was a pure genius going to school."

When I changed nations, suddenly
I became the oldest: I don't know how.
And now there is only one category
In which I can hope to be surprisingly young:
"He can't have been fifty. But they all
Died young, the Donoghues. If his father
Was fifty, he wasn't much more than it."

Thirty years back. By now his being dead
Is by no means prodigious, after he
Changed states that cold March. And whether
This maturing should make us
More reconciled or sadder
Is extremely hard to say.

SUN LIFE OF CANADA
for my sisters

What made us special in our early days
Was their free publicity material:
Christmas cards of Mounties; bright pink
Blotting-paper with snow-capped hills
On the back; small celluloid calenders
Most of all, that flared blinding blue
When we dropped them, having switched off
The light, on the front-room fire.

All day at school we yearned for them:
That, having trudged through the rushy fields
Of soaked lady's smock and primroses
In the shadow of our cloudy mountains,
We might sit before the fire, dreaming
Of that sun life beneath a sheer blue sky,
Which, since we had pictures of it,
We might in due course live.

Those days of rain and flowers. Knowing
The value of money changes, we're no longer
Blinded so lightly; but we still recall
Uneasily warnings about the waste
Of burning calenders. Time is money,
Money time. That's all we seem to know.

ROMANTIC LOVE

I've never felt the same about your eyes
Since learning that it's superfluity
Of uric acid that causes their brownness.
If that is true, then the small sticking-plaster
Folded in your elegant right elbow
May not be what you say it is – the cover
Of a hole made in your vein by the needle
Of the blood-doctor – but the calculated
Seal of your addiction.

I'd have your brown eyes blue:
Blue as lobelia, or expensive iris,
Or as the night sky over London,
Or the light on the dashboard
That indicates the headlights are full on.

SECOND-CLASS RELICS

"Pilgrimage to Lourdes from Ireland is not to
  be classed as foreign travel and therefore should
  not require a passport"
      (Tadhg Foley)

When John Tim Jack made his pilgrimage
To Lourdes, he never got as far
As filling the neighbours' bottles
With the healing waters, so on the way home
He stopped at the stream in Islandbrack
And filled them there. Grace and recognition
Followed just the same. In every household
The clear bottles shook a blessing
On the youngsters driving irresponsibly
To dances at the *Mecca Ballroom*
Or the *Edel Quinn*. Its efficacy
Seemed no less than the pink-crossed window
Of linen that had touched the bones
Of Philomena, or the Aero-like
Volcanic rock we brought from Iceland,
Or the chippings from the Berlin Wall
You see on many travellers' mantelpieces
These days. All are prayed to; who's to say
The water where the cattle wash their feet
Is not as curative as that where saints
Appear, or that the New Order will not start
Below the bridge where John Tim's pups were drowned?

'EBBE?'

She used to say. Was always. Didn't like.
Such cold, novel preterites: not long since
She is and thinks and says. Always positive,
Active voice, imperfect, running with buckets.

On her birthday now my work goes well.
I don't need to get hot and irritated
Combing the unending remainder shelves
For Namier or the loves of Charles the Second.
She isn't waiting to enthuse too much
While warming to her theme, her eyes lighter blue
As she expanded, dwelling on the page.

Now I'd welcome the tedium of her History's
Excessive circumstantiality.
In this future perfect I wouldn't sigh.

OTTER-CHILDREN

Where did I leave my cap? Some day
I must look. Maybe in the room
Where the stuffed otter twists to face you
In his cage of water. Once I or someone
Stood with a homemade dragnet,
Kneedeep, shifting in the river
After a flood, hoping to catch
The salmon and with him (who knows?)
Wisdom. I watched a dark shape
Speed downstream, then hit square on,
Causing me to lose footing.
And hat and bag and tackle.

The last time I ventured in the room
(You'll come in to look?) I thought I saw,
Hiding behind the arching couch,
Children – two, even three – laughing
And sly. When you look straight at them,
You see nothing. But when you face
The humbled water-dog's indignant glare,
You can sense them, like a migraine's shiver
In the top lefthand corner of your vision,
Laughing still but also holding out
A hand pleading with you to step across
The firescreen, into their day beyond.

THE GREAT FAMINE

It's a bit Irish, you well might think,
That the term for it translates as
'The great place of tillage-fields'.
But it's apt enough; along the paths
Were fragrant woodbine hedges
And beautiful, inedible dog-roses,
Made to flourish by the same hot damp
That caused the crops to putrefy.

In Skibbereen, a smiling farmer tells
Tourists stories about the Famine.
"People used to gather down at the point
To watch the coffin-ships passing westward
To America. My own grandfather
Had an *Examiner* from the eighteen-fifties,
Advertising the better quarters
As having five feet clearance between decks."

Feeling the first drops, he opens out
A huge golf-umbrella: red and green
And white and blue and orange, sighing
"This would be a great country if
We only had the weather." A farmer
Distinguishes past years by weather;
And he hungers most for the seasoning
That salts with glamour the old taste of failure.

NEIGHBOURHOOD WATCH

The tinkers live beyond the verges
Of the town. Under cover of night
Their dogs scavenge from the dustbins,
Knocking the lids off. In broad daylight
They tether their ponies by our hedges.

The shopkeepers live lives of their own.
They pull down the blinds at 9 p.m.
To count their takings behind locked doors.
Their children often die before their parents
While business is creamed off by supermarkets.

The people live in the better parts of town,
With long lawns and variegated borders
Stretching down to the lane. They used to take
The tinkers' children in service by the year,
But now they're warier and make their own beds.

CLOSE ENCOUNTERS

The tern-acrobats were the warm-up act
Before the shore finally drew away
And the pelagic main feature began:
First fulmars; then gannets in ones
And pairs and, this year, two sevens
In geeselike formations. Just past halfway
We saw a petrel, living in its sea-pit
Close to the water, a small instrument
We strained for from the gods. Shearwaters
Were the stars, turning from black
To white with even-handedness.

It was a good haul and all were happy
To go inside. We'd just begun to think
Of whether it was necessary to eat again
Before disembarkation when the engines
Were dwarfed by a coarser roar alongside.
All went back on deck to see it:
A yellow RAF helicopter, flappering
Just overhead, seeming almost in reach.
Next, from its door a man appeared
And, turning slowly on his invisible spit,
Sank past the deck in his outrider's leathers.

He swung past us and disappeared
Into the hull below. But not for long:
Soon he was out again and caught himself
On the helicopter's fishing-line
To be reeled in. His last performance
Was to stand at the door and wave
In acknowledgment of his audience.
And there we were: Irish of the first
And second and third generation,
Applauding his showmanship before
His great container swung away towards base.

GOING WITHOUT SAYING
i.m. Joe Flynn

It is a great pity we don't know
When the dead are going to die
So that, over a last companionable
Drink, we could tell them
How much we liked them.

Happy the man who, dying, can
Place his hand on his heart and say:
"At least I didn't neglect to tell
The thrush how beautifully she sings."

THE YEAR WE DISCOVERED SCENERY

A railway-line that stopped
Over the sea first set us
Thinking as we looked
Northwest towards Dingle, till
At last the mist lifted
And we could run the length
Of the strand under Been Hill.

It was the year I first took
Photographs; I had no filters
So I couldn't catch you
Silhouetted, stooping
To examine a crab
In the blinding red
Of the evening's low rays.

All through the dark I built
Your face, imagining
A dry sandcastle, desperately
Coaxed upwards with the palms,
Or a jigsaw that never made
A picture: just as now
These lines can't capture it again.

A GOOD CONSTITUTION

*"I apologize for whatever it is in me that
brings out the worst in you"* (Albee)

Because we are not hamstrung by a charter
Or written constitution, we're at liberty
To choose our freedoms. Here's one I'd enshrine:

That every decent person have the right
To look on every side and only find
What pleases him or her: green fields,
Sunshine, diving swallows, old folks
Cycling to evensong, occasionally
Merrying their silvery bells
At sparrows ruffling in the roadside dust.

By a similar provision they'd be free
Only to have good news: to never see
Naked crying children running at the camera,
Their family villages burning at their backs,
Or beggars in their silly cardboard houses
Whose drug-blurred voices spoil that rare night out,
Echoing in the overpass above the concert hall.

THE ROBIN IN AUTUMN

He's watched the prizewinners,
One by one, taking off
For their world tour, until
At last he's top of the bill.
Without the competition
Of the blackcap, his lyric
From the leaves is as good
As anyone's, even becoming
Indistinguishable from the champions
In the ear's memory. In due course
The leaves themselves will fly
And he'll stand out alone
On the bare rostrum
Of his Christmas card.

WHITE ELEPHANTS

I love the fruits of our technology:
The CD, the Volvo, the washing aids.
But my heart bleeds for those less
Fortunate, who starve or lack
Even the most basic amenities.
By a curious quirk of fate (have you
Ever pondered this?) it's they too
Who are liable to earthquakes.
There but for the grace of God go
I, say I. A 10p in your box.

Not that there aren't recently
Some disquieting signs.
Was our weather always as dry
As this? In those loved, lost days
Of youth I can't remember
The grass disappearing, or cracks
Across the fields. Not that I'd want
To precipitate panic buying
Or anything of that sort.
But another coin in the box.

It's hardly surprising of course:
The traffic queues extend for miles
And you can hardly get to the beach.
Sooner or later they'll have to introduce
Legislation. In the mean time
I've taken to driving through
The hours of night, watching the blue
Roadsigns glow by, adjusting
With finger-tip control my favourite
Discs. A penny for your thoughts.

GRIEF SUSPENDED

As denser liquids hang suspended
In the more rarefied, appearing solid,
So does grief hang in our air
Like worms of setting toffee,
Congealing in water. Even when
It half-dissolves, it smears
The surface, forming a viscid
Solution that's unfit to drink.

Once it's happened, you're never
The same again, fearing to gulp in
Draughts of air lest its invisible
Compound might contain traces,
Like De Selby's motes of darkness,
From grief's crematorium-chimney.

ÁINE

i.m. Áine Murphy who died aged 5 months

Those rosebuds I brought away
From the room in the crematorium
Where your small white coffin
Slid from view, wilted
On the car's plastic ledge
While we ate and drank, all of us,
Mourning your taking-off.
But two days later, look,
They're reaching up again
On a sunny windowsill,
Learning to stand
On stems, frail and graceful,
Pink bowls unbalanced
With perfect unease
On their long, green shoots.

FIGHTING OVER THE WATER

It's not very likely that we
Won't fight to the last drop
Of water, considering how
We've fought throughout the ages,
Greatly finding quarrel
In every square yard of land.

But that's what they tell us:
That, while we watch the green earth
Browning under unrelenting sun,
We'll close ranks: that when death
Threatens, we'll help each other out
Better than usual.

It reminds me of Paddy Fitz
On Korea: "They're fighting again
Over the water." Wars were abroad:
Our part to comb the hay's tresses,
Moulding the ricks' roofs against rain,
Or to make unlikely earthen shelters

For potato-pits. Can we believe
That tears, inner and outer,
Will be all we bring to the husting?
Or that their saltiness won't dry
More than they vivify? Can we trust
The desalination plant at the cliff-edge?

WHAT'S THE TIME, MR WOLF?

Glass, someone once told me, is a liquid
Of such density that its sluggish
Downward seep takes centuries to work,
So medieval windows are thicker
At the bottom than the top. If I push

My index-finger up along the bridge
Of my nose, I smooth away the wrinkles
I recall erasing with the same
(But smaller) finger from my mother's forehead
Forty years back, spiriting her frown away.

Have you noticed when you stand erect,
Breathing in, how your chest-flesh has
A tendency to droop towards the floor,
More markedly with every year
That passes? It creeps for the earth,

Like a child in a race stealing more odds
While the starter's back is turned,
Or the Pardoner's old man, tapping
The ground with his stick and pleading
"Dear mother, let me in."

METAMORPHOSIS

A flower of spring, the lupin's gone by June.
Theresa brought them to us in four glass jars
On her way to school, and we planted them
Due west of the house. They were dwarf variety
With small pink and yellow flowers,
But twenty years later they were portly,
Swelling bushes, eighteen years after
Theresa herself had died of polio.

Now that another decade's passed, her children
Would be going to school and the dry seeds
That cracked in the pods refulgent,
So I have the heart to try again my hand
At lupins. And every morning, back here
In Knockduff, I'm woken at 4 a.m.
By a single agitated swallow,
Patrolling her alarm-calls up and down

The yard. When I pull the curtains open,
I can just make her out, flying fast
In wide ellipses, as if practising
For the long haul to Africa. Finally,
She alights straight overhead, her anxious
Insistent twitters settling into
The grace of a happy end with the fiddler's
Leaning down on the second-last note.